That Shakespeherian Rag

That Shakespeherian Rag

Poems by

Edmund Conti

© 2021 Edmund Conti. All rights reserved.
This material may not be reproduced in any form, published,
reprinted, recorded, performed, broadcast,
rewritten or redistributed without
the explicit permission of Edmund Conti.
All such actions are strictly prohibited by law.

Cover design by Shay Culligan
Cover art by Edmund Conti

ISBN: 978-1-954353-99-2

Kelsay Books
502 South 1040 East, A-119
American Fork, Utah, 84003
Kelsaybooks.com

For Marilyn

Who loved poetry and "liked" some of my poems.

Acknowledgments

The following poems were previously published where noted:

Abbey: "Losing Battle," "Moonlighting."
Better Than Starbucks: "Home Suite."
Cat's Eye: "On Writing Light Verse."
Ed C. Scrolls: "Agreeable," "In the Beginning was the F-word."
Hic Haiku Hoc: "The Party's Over."
Hobo Stew Review: "Balls."
Humerus: "Spring Song."
Light: "Light at the End of the Tunnel," "Frostfree," "Rinse Cycle," "Three Haiku Embedded," "Two's Company," "Button Button," "Now I Lay Me Down to Sleep," "Footsteps," "The Secret Life of Butterflies," "Cravat Emptor," "Pillage Rape Plunder," "On Becoming a Famous Poet," "An Island Entire," "Elements of Surprise," "Bob and Weave."
Lighten-up Online: "One Fine Day," "A Ulysses You'll Like."
Muse: "A Musing."
NOO Journal: "Clean Laundry on the Stairs."
NY Sunday Times (NJ edition): "Outpouring."
Opossum Holler Tarot: "Open Frame."
Orphic Lute: "Job and M&M's."
Paterson Literary Review: "My Frank Sinatra Poem."
Plastic Tower: "Regeneration," "A Lovely Day in the Neighborhood."
Slugfest: "Pray Go," "Dante's Inferno," "My Son, the Critic."
Small Pond: "How to Write a Sestina."
Sow's Ear: "Bull!"
Stone Drum: "Memory."
The Lyric: "The Road to Hell."
The Quarterly: "Lost in Translation."
Verse-Virtual: "Me and Billy Collins," "Coming Home," "Dramatis Personae," "Poetry in Motion," "Tabled," "Time and Tide."

Contents

1

Cereal Killers	19
I 80	21
Light at the End of the Tunnel	22
Loner	23
The Maltese Falcon	24
Me and Billy Collins	25
My Frank Sinatra Poem	26

2

A Ulysses You'll Like	29
Witness	31
Frostfree	32
The Love Song of J. Billy Collins	33
Two Cities in Two Minutes	34
Hamlet in a Hurry	35
One Fine Day	36
Ring Cycle, Rinse Cycle, Repeat	37

3

Balls	41
A Brief History of Time and the River	42
The Elements of Surprise	43
Love for Sale	44
I'll Take a Raincheck	45
Pray Go	46
Three Haiku Embedded in a Classic Light Verse Quatrain	47
Open Frame	48

4

Job and the Amazing Technicolor M&M's	51
Two's Company	52
Dante's Inferno	53
In the Beginning Was the F-word	54
Agreeable	55
In the Beginning Was the Last Word	56
The Road to Hell Is Paved with Good Intentions	57

5

How to Write a Sestina	61
Bob and Weave	63
Button, Button	64
Memory	65
Outpouring	66
On Writing Light Verse	67

6

Coming Home	71
Clean Laundry on the Stairs	72
Dramatis Personae	73
Home Suite	74
My Son the Critic	75
Poetry in Motion	77
Losing Battle	78
Regeneration	79
Now I Lay Me Down to Sleep	80
Footsteps	81

7

Bad Day at Black Rock	85
Rain Date	86
Short Attention Span	87
An Epistle from Paul	88
Bull!	89
The Secret Life of Butterflies	90
Vegetarians	91

8

Cravat Emptor	95
Benediction	96
Pillage, Rape, Plunder; Pillage, Rape, Plunder	97
Excitement	98
Bend It Like Edmund	99
Differential Calculus	100
Lost in Translation	101
Id Est	102

9

Live from the Sidewalk, It's Me!	105
A Lovely Day in the Neighborhood	106
Beaming	107
Moonlighting	108
A Musing	109
Speaking for Ourselves, Ann	110
Spring Song	111
The Straight Skinny	112
Tabled	113
Shoot for the Moon	114

10

On Becoming a Famous Poet	117
Shadows, 9–10–200	118
The War of the Roses Comes to an Exciting Anti-Climax	119
Time and Tide	120
An Island Entire of Myself	121
Spoiler	122
The Party's Over	123

11

O O O O that Shakespeherean rag
 It's so elegant
 So intelligent

—T. S. Eliot, *The Waste Land*

1

True it is that we have seen better days.

—As You Like It
Act II Scene 7

Cereal Killers

Kids, remember Tom Mix at six?
No, it must have been at five.
Six was for supper. Remember supper?

When the whole family sat down to eat
together. And if you didn't like what
was served, too bad. You could just sit there

until bedtime. But back to Tom Mix.
And Jack Armstrong. And their announcers.
Kids, they would say. You wouldn't eat cold eggs

for breakfast. Then why eat cold cereal?
Have a nice hot breakfast of Ralston Farina.
Still, we hardly ever ate eggs for breakfast, hot

or cold. Maybe once in a while my father
would make his famous scrambled eggs,
eggshells and all. But back to the radio.

Or as they would say, Meanwhile back at the ranch.
Or Hudson High School. Of course
we listened to the commercials. Everything

on the radio was magic. Besides there was no
mute button. Unless you turned off the radio.
But we didn't want to miss anything. Not even

the announcer for Jack Armstrong saying, Kids,
you don't heat up the coal before you shovel it
into the furnace. But then I never shoveled coal

into our furnace. My father wouldn't let me.
I was never the All-American boy.
I never ate cold Wheaties for breakfast.

I 80

I'm driving down Interstate 80
minding my own business at a safe
and sensible 45 miles per hour
with my right directional blinking
which I don't notice because I'm
thinking about other things like
writing this poem and besides I
don't hear the bink-bink-bink be-
cause I have high-tone deafness
and I don't pay attention to
the horns blowing behind me and
the headlights flashing but I do
notice the 2 cars on either side
of me decide to meet in the lane
(my lane) in front of me and I
have to slow down to avoid them
(stupid New Jersey drivers)
but they interrupt my train of
thought and anyway I have to
finish this later because there's
                              my
                                      exit.

Light at the End of the Tunnel

When I was one and twenty
A wise man said to me
If you want to be a poet
Make sure your verse is free.
But I was in my salad days
It was the best of times
I thought I could out-Ogden Nash.
I wanted to make rhymes.

When I was two and twenty
He said to bite the bullet, Sir,
If you want to be in "Poetry"
Or win a prize from Pulitzer.
And now with no poems weighty
And most of them in "Light"
I've reached the age of eighty
And oh, he's right, he's right.

Loner

Al Shdeed indeed. A guy I knew.
Indeed, I did! Back in Junior High.
I think he was a Syrian, something like that.
No, not Assyrian. We studied them
in Ancient History. Though he had a big nose
like their pictures in the school books.
A real beak. But that was no problem.
Our school was filled with Italians and Armenians.
So Al and his name and his nose didn't stand out.
Not with guys like Shabab Shababian. No sir,
we didn't care that Al was an Arab. (Truth is,
we didn't know.) So we accepted him, that is,
they accepted him They never
accepted me.

The Maltese Falcon

Everyone asks
you're Italian
how come you don't
know the difference
between Al Pacino
and Robert De Niro?

I tell them
I'm Maltese
and I'm a poet.

They laugh and ask
Where's your rhymes?

Me and Billy Collins

The sun, low on the horizon,
is streaming through the window.
The northeast is suffering one
of its worst cold spells in years.
(They always say that, these
meteorologists with short memories.)
I'm cozy here and warm, the iMac
purring away, iTunes bringing me
Rosemary Clooney, her voice mellow,
years away from "Come On A My
House." I am trying to write a poem.

And I'm thinking of Billy Collins.
What would he make of my
little corner of the world.
Would he make more of it
if I had a small crate of oranges
nearby? Or a book on Stalin…

Billy—can I call you that, Mr. Collins?—
And you can call me…What?
Eddie? Ed? Edmund? Edward?
(I get a lot of that.) Tell you what—
call me Conti and I'll call you Collins.
Just imagine, if I were a little younger
I would have sat behind you in grammar school.
We could have passed notes. In verse!
We could have bonded and—who knows—
I could have been the famous poet now.
And you? You could be writing this poem.

My Frank Sinatra Poem

Miss Trifari stretched her five-foot
two-inch body to reach the top of the blackboard
where she wrote out *agricola* (farmer, masculine,
singular, nominative case). She followed that
with *agricolae* (genitive case, of the farmer).
She continued to labor at the blackboard until
she had declined "farmer" in all five cases,
singular and plural. I, of course, decline to spell
out all the variations. I was good at Latin but
all I remember now are the names of the cases—
nominative, genitive, dative, accusative, ablative.
And the ablative absolute. How I loved the ablative
absolute! The farmer having sowed, the fields
were ready to reap.   But what I really remember
were the tests. Miss Trifari would pass out
the corrected tests and make us read our marks
to the class. I remember one day in Latin class
at Nathanael Greene Junior High School. A cold
wet winter day in 1942, the rain turning to snow.
I was daydreaming, looking out the window into
the future. The marks were being read—72, 81
67, 76, 79. Gray marks for a gray day. I don't know
how we were seated, but it wasn't alphabetically
since Arthur Schwartz sat in front of me. Maybe
it was by height, although I have the feeling that
Arthur was taller than me. Anyway, I was one
of the last to read my score. When my turn came
I blurted out "97." There were gasps and screams
from the whole class. Like I said, I was good in Latin.
Then. Arthur Schwartz, bless his 13-year-old heart,
turned around to me with a gleam in his eyes and
in his best imitation of a swooning bobbysoxer
screamed out "Frankie!"

2

The moon's an arrant thief, and her pale fire
she snatches from the sun.

—Timon of Athens
Act IV Scene 3

A Ulysses You'll Like

People who tell you that reading's for sissies
Were never assigned James Joyce's Ulysses.

The Law tried to help you by calling it porn
But a learned District Judge merely viewed that with scorn.

As for the sex scenes, the book seems to need them.
However, our judge notes, you don't have to read them.

Since the sex is redeeming and therefore might bore you.
I made it my mission to read the book for you.

The first page says only these words "Stately plump"
If you get through that then you're over the hump.

Starting off with a large capital "S"
And finishing, yes, with a capitalized "Yes."

And in between those, just what have you got?
Leopold Bloom wandering, wandering, that's what.

It's June the sixteenth in Dublin fair (and ugly).
Oh yes, you say, Bloomsday. (Don't say it so smugly.)

Wandering and wandering and wandering, you see
That it's kind of like an Odyssey.

Meanwhile, Readers, home raising the ante,
Hugh "Blazes" Boylan has Molly flagrante.

Bloom's doing Dublin so it hardly amazes
That Leopold's Molly is going to Blazes.

Glad that you missed this? Here is my guess.
Yes, I think, Yes, I know, Yes, indeed, Yes.

Witness

You heard a fly buzz—when you died—
You were still in the room—
I said I wasn't there—I lied—
I came to share your doom.

I meant to fly around and leave
But someone said it was you.
I thought—therefore—that I should grieve
But first—for fun—I'd buzz you.

So here I fly—just interposing
In your poem to make a hash of—
But here is Death—I must be closing.
And now—Miss D.—I'll dash off.

Frostfree

The land was ours before we were the land's.
It used to be the other way around
But that is something no one understands.

Before we start let's have a show of hands,
Does anyone regard this as profound?
The land was ours before we were the land's.

The argument we're stating here demands
That each of us commits to stand his ground
But that is something no one understands.

The footing's tricky—watch the shifting sands
As well as arguments that may astound.
The land was ours before we were the land's.

We seem to be at sea between two strands
To sink or swim and possibly be drowned
But that is something no one understands.

Two final thoughts before this poem disbands
(does anybody want another round?):
The land was ours before we were the land's.
But that is something no one understands.

The Love Song of J. Billy Collins

You are the diner in sawdust restaurants,
the other woman in one-night cheap hotels.
You are one of those women talking of Michelangelo
and Rembrandt and Picasso and Klee.
You are the woman who dares to eat a peach
or even mangoes and over-ripe bananas.

However, you are not a pair of ragged claws,
and, dear, you never scuttle.
Nor do you shimmy, slither or sashay.
And you are certainly not the confidant of Ezra Pound.
There is no way you could be the confidant of Ezra Pound.

It might interest you to know,
speaking of mandarin oranges and things poetical,
that I am not Prince Hamlet
or any other Great Dane you might know.

But I am the yellow smoke that glides along the street
and the patient etherized upon a table.
But don't worry, I am not the diner in sawdust restaurants.
You are still the diner in the restaurant.
You will always be the diner in the restaurant.
Not to mention the sawdust on the floor and—somehow—the
cheap white wine.

Two Cities in Two Minutes

Life was hard in Bourbon France
Peasants didn't have a chance.

The royal court would gormandize
And the nobles weren't any prize.

Meanwhile back in England, merry
Things were better, but not very.

No guillotines, no Defarge knittin'
No Bourbon here, it's Scotch in Britain.

Our tale unfolds in perilous times
With the best of rhymes and the worst of rhymes.

Doctor Manette was put away.
Have a nice, they said, Bastille Day.

Daughter Lucie lives in London
Trying hard not to come undone.

Returns to France with Charles Darnay.
He's French and should have stayed away.

He's a former noble, *mise en scene*
And is headed for the guillotine.

Wait! here's our hero, Carton, Sydney.
Well, he wanted to be a hero, didn'e?
Takes Charles' place, the plot gets juicy.
Pourquoi? you ask. "Moi, I love Lucie."

But shed no tears, our hero shines,
Reciting the world's best closing lines.

Hamlet in a Hurry

To be or not to be
Hamlet of Elsinore
Father dead, uncle king
He felt bereft.

Crazily did in the
Dramatis personae
Characteristic'ly
No one was left.

One Fine Day

See Butterfly
Go flutter by
Her manner is *shibui*
Her vigil night
A symphonic delight
And made your eyes all dewy.

Her melody
Un Bella Di
(Or is it "Bel?" Whatever.)
I'm ill at ease
In Japanese
(Italian? How clever!)

But soon she slept
As we were swept
Away by all the passion
Her ship came in
Oh no, you nin-
compoop! Not in that fashion.

Lieutenant Pink-
erton, the fink,
Has come, but brought a bride
O Cho-Cho San
You can't go on
Not when there's suicide.

Oh, East is East
And West is West
And when the twain do meet
It's the kind of stuff
O opera buff
To keep you in your seat.

Ring Cycle, Rinse Cycle, Repeat

Hibbity-hobbity
J.R.R. Tolkien
Penned the adventures of
Frodo and friends.

Uninterruptedly
Told of their journey in
Book after book after
Book till it ends.

3

O, that is entertainment.
My bosom likes it not, nor my brows.

—The Winter's Tale
Act I Scene 2

Balls

ground air
low high
moth fly
butter gutter
bouncing bowling
golf basket soccer volley (golly!)

fast curve
foul fair
gum eye knuckle hand foot
hair pin
meat squash corn bean

                                                           hidden

eight nine tennis
dead black snow
dirt dust scum spit sleaze
cannon fire RACQUET
Billy punch

brass brass

A Brief History of Time and the River

. . . .of expanding forever and the universe again. . .
of space-time, black holes and the mellow-sounding
quark. And of the big bang, the rich bang,
the strange unknown bang.

Where shall the universe rest? When shall
the lonely galaxies come home? What planets
are open for the astronaut? And which of us
shall find his, farther away, know its orbit,
and in what star system, and in what continuum,
and in what dimension? Where? Where the weary
of prosody can hide forever, where the weary of
pastiche can find peace, where the poet-manqué,
the poetaster and the versifier can be forever
stilled.

The Elements of Surprise

I have no favorites. I love them all.
Start with actinium; end with zirconium.
Along the way give each one an encomium—
The elements displayed against the wall.

Hydrogen and helium you see.
Atomic numbers one and two. They perch
Astride the periodic table. No search
Required. Left H. Right He. Hi H. Hi He.

O look! there's oxygen and B for boron.
Some elements have symbols that may trouble you.
Potassium is K and tungsten? W!
And who made mercury Hg. Some moron?

Not I. And not John Donne. Like him I write
"Of elements and an angelic sprite."

Love for Sale

I love you, O Auberon Waugh,
Although I cannot tell you orally
For your last name it sticks in my craw
And it may be I'm rhyming immorally.

I love you, O Auberon Waugh.
I love with a love that is lawless.
I love every last little flaw
(Assuming, of course, you're not flawless.)

I love you, O Auberon Waugh,
With a love that wants more than a bright rhyme.
I love how I hope you will laugh
When you happen upon that last sight rhyme.

I love you, O Auberon Waugh.
It's the sound of your name that I revel in.
I once loved your Maw or your Paw
(Whichever of them was called Evelyn.)

I love you, O Auberon Waugh.
Oh my love please, O Auberon Waugh, be.
Is your Englishness starting to thaw?
If it is then may I call you Aubie?

I love you! I love you! I love you!
You are warm. You are wise. And exciting.
So, how could I feel less of you—
Who passed away during this writing.

I'll Take a Raincheck

No matter
how topical
the typical
tropical
rain forest,
it isn't for me
the ultimately
plain tourist.

Pray Go

Is Prego better than Ragu?
Is Ragu better than Prego?
Is Togo close to the Congo?
Would Hugo be seen in a Yugo?
Would you go to Chicago?
To the Volga with Helga?
With a Virgo, amigo?
To San Diego, Montago,
Santiago with Maggie?
In a toga? In an igloo?
Would Hoagie? Would Bogie?
Would they boogie with Peggy?
With a pygmy? In a buggy?
Play bingo with Ringo?
Or would the stigma, the enigma,
The alph and omega,
The dogma, the saga,
Make them go gaga?
For reggae?
For Pogo in Pago Pago?
Would you forgo four goats?
For the Big O?
    Ergo
Prego is better than Ragu.
Ragu is better than Prego.

Three Haiku Embedded in a Classic Light Verse Quatrain

Before you said, "Have more ragout,"

> Blowing snow outside
> Kitchen aromas inside
> Warm yourself with soup.

And let the cat inside the bag out,

> Cat fills window sill
> Soaking up all the sunshine
> Greedy animal!

I was an ignoramus who

> Moonlight finds the fox.
> Cherry blossoms, the hedgehog.
> So what do I know?

Had always said, "Please pass the rag-out."

Open Frame

Bowling
May not
be a yup-
pie sport
I mean yr
teammates
might be
Betty or
Slim and
al- though
the lanes
are fast
it's not
the fast
lane if
you know
what I
mean but
it's real
and some-
times it
ends up
like this:

7   10

4

There are more things in Heaven and Earth,
Horatio, than are dreamt of in your philosophy.

—Hamlet
Act I Scene 5

Job and the Amazing Technicolor M&M's

I like the pretty little fellows
The oranges, the greens and yellows
I even like the tan.
But when I want to down one
I always grab a brown one
According to God's plan.

Two's Company

Sweet are the uses of divinity
And sweeter yet in keeping us engrossed
Is the simple complex concept of the trinity
The Father, Son and Holy Ghost.

Is making sense of Them too much a bother?
Is there any way to master Three-in-One?
The Son, the Holy Ghost and Father,
The Holy Ghost, the Father and the Son.

I use this ancient form, the cranky sonnet
To crank out my aberrant Dunciad
And what evolves from overthinking on it:
The Spook, the Kid and—dare I say it?—Dad.

It's true that poems are made by fools like me
But only God can make himself a three.

Dante's Inferno

I read the whole of it
Just for the Hell of it.

In the Beginning Was the F-word

And God said
be fruitful
and multiply
but don't
talk about it.

Agreeable

Amen
to all
amen-
ties.

In the Beginning Was the Last Word

According to my erstwhile
Bible (or was it just something I heard?)
The first shall be last
               and the last first, while
The antepenultimate shall be third.

The Road to Hell Is Paved with Good Intentions

Tried.
Fried.

5

Words, words, words.

—Hamlet
Act II Scene 2

How to Write a Sestina

The idea is to use only simple words
To end each of your six required lines.
Allowing you to get the most use from them.
For instance, use multi-purpose words like 'body'
And avoid one-function ones like 'braggadocio'
That are used to, say, block on third and long.

Remember that a sestina is overly long—
Six time six lines is a lot of words.
You're going to need all your braggadocio
To get through this. There will be lines
And wrinkles all over your poet's body.
And every day you'll see more of them.

Hey, two stanzas! Just need four more of them.
Plus an envoi. Which is only half as long.
We can do this as well as anybody.
Humming along though we know the words.
We're pleasing our readers but the bottom line's
Where we have to profit from braggadocio.

By now we know how to spell 'braggadocio'
And 'sestina'—good Italian words like them
Will help you get in a few good lines
At your next cocktail party, jumping headlong
Into witty conversation with your new-found words
That are guaranteed to impress somebody.

You need a healthy mind in a healthy body
Unless, of course, you're Felix Braggadocio,
A man of brute strength and few words.
I'm a nose tackle, he says, who needs them?
But professional football careers are not long
Especially playing in the defensive lines.

Completing this won't keep you out of the bread lines.
(Poetry has never nourished the body.)
But that's the short run—in the long,
Command of the language, a little braggadocio
And a flair for the obvious makes you one of them,
The movers and the shakers. Mark my words.

Well, there's thirty-six lines of braggadocio.
I think we need an anti-body for them.
Something long on wit and short on words.

Bob and Weave

I asked my friend, the poet, Bob,
Say, what exactly do you do?
I scribble poems, he said. My job.
That's what I do. And you?

I told him that I offered crits
On poems that needed critting.
He eyed me like I was the pits
And went back to his knitting.

Undaunted by this tactic, I
Resumed the conversation.
I thought I'd give it one more try
To bring this guy salvation.

Oh, some are saved and some are not
And many are not craving
Salvation from a monoglot.
They don't think they need saving.

So Bob the poet carries on
Ignoring all the critters
Who fall their rusty swords upon
And drink their pint of bitters.

Now, East is East and West is West
And the corn (ahem) is on the cob.
And all of us still stay impressed
By the word according to Bob.

Button, Button

When one subtracts from life infancy
(which is vegetation),—sleep, eating, and swilling
buttoning and unbuttoning—how much remains of
downright existence?
   —The Summer of a Dormouse, Byron's Journals

Just ask the poet, life's a dumb thing.
Button, button, eating, swilling.
Life isn't much but, still, it's something.

Existence is a rule-of-thumb thing.
Buying now with later billing.
Just ask the poet, life's a dumb thing.

To dream, to sleep, a ho-and-hum thing.
Boring, boring, mulling, milling.
Life isn't much but, still, it's something.

Mum's the word, the word's a mum thing.
Button lips and no bean spilling.
Just ask the poet, life's a dumb thing.

Life, of course—the known-outcome thing.
Death and taxes. God is willing.
Life isn't much but, still, it's something.

Life is short, a bit-of-crumb thing.
Dormouse summer, daddies grilling.
Just ask the poet, life's a dumb thing.
Life isn't much but, still, it's something.

Memory

It's full of lots of little bits
Structured so that each one fits
Which are recalled, retrieved or gotten
(Unless, of course, they're just forgotten).
Stored up in an oubliette
For getting what you should forget.

Outpouring

The dam was flawed.
It overflowed.
So me and Floyd—
We fled the flood.

On Writing Light Verse

Here's what I find
When I'm mopping the floor—
Oh, never mind,
It's been all done before.

6

A little more than kin, and less than kind.

—Hamlet
Act II Scene 2

Coming Home

Dad has boarded the bus with a bottle
of beer and some potato chips. He settles
in and pulls out the cell phone. Meanwhile
in the kitchen back home, Mom has burnt
the macaroni and cheese and is considering,
among other things, Kraft. Lisa is crying
in the highchair and has swept all the Cheerios
to the floor. Oh, did I mention
the breakfast dishes, they haven't
been washed yet. Timmy, where's Timmy?
Yep, there he is, jumping up and down
in the laundry basket. And why is the cat…
wait, we don't have a cat. Do we?
Millie is quietly doing her homework
at the kitchen table. Millie is quiet.
The cartoon she is watching on TV isn't.
Ah, there's the phone. Hello.
Millie, talk to your dad.
He's on the bus.

Clean Laundry on the Stairs

As my son
climbed over
the laundry

basket
first the right
sneakered foot

then the left
skirted this
obstacle

on the way
to his
bedroom.

Dramatis Personae

I show this poem to my wife
and she says do you have to say
fuck it's not your style and I say
—to myself—fuck, I'm not going
to show her any more poems, and
—to her—it's necessary
to the sense of the poem and be-
sides it's not me it's my persona.
What's a persona? She asks.
It's the voice of the poem, I explain,
the speaker, the someone
who's saying these things and
I, the poet, declaim them,
like an actor.

Act your age, she says.

Home Suite

This place along the road I call my home—
The house that's on the corner by the school,
The house from which I said I'd never roam,
The house that in the backyard has no pool.

The house that has more bed rooms than we need
And half as many bathrooms (clean and bright).
Where both my sons when little often peed
And as their aim got better got it right.

A fireplace that works, an eat-in kitchen,
A dining room where dining was aloud,
Our cozy porch, a glassed-in jewel, which in
Summer, spring or autumn did us proud.

Where what we saved on heating filled our coffer.
Where memories still linger. Make an offer.

My Son the Critic

Read me a bedtime poem, said my son.
So I read him this:

We say hippopotami
But not rhinoceri
A strange dichotomy
In nature's glossary.

But we do say rhinoceri, he said. Look it up.
So I read him this:

Life is unfair
For most of us, therefore
Let's have a fanfare
For those that it's fair for.

I smell a slant rhyme, he said, sniffing.
So I read him this:

While trying to grapple
With gravity, Newton
Was helped by an apple
He didn't compute on.

My teacher says that's not poetry, he said.
So I read him this:

René Descartes, he thought
And therefore knew he was.
And since he was, he sought
To make us think. He does.

That made me think, he said. But not feel.
So I read him this:

My hair has a wonderful sheen.
My toenails, clipped, have regality.
It's just all those things in between
That give me a sense of mortality.

Did the earth move? I asked. Anything?
Nothing moved. He was asleep.

Poetry in Motion

Just look at that beautiful star
exclaims my wife, pointing haphazardly
at the northeast quadrant of that inverted bowl
we more prosaic souls call the sky.
Which one, I ask, showing off. Betelgeuse?
Alpha Centauri? Polaris? That one, there,
right over the telephone pole. I try to explain
to her that my star over the telephone pole
is not the same as hers. But parallax
is best consummated in daylight
between consenting adults. I try again.
Do you mean Sirius, I ask, pointing out
the bright star in the constellation Orion.
Get serious, she laughs, and I know this will be
a night to remember. My wife has made a joke.

And you have made a poem! I would have her say.
But she doesn't. And I haven't. And the stars,
the stars spin as one around the Pole.
And all of us—the stars, my wife, her joke,
the telephone pole and me—are hurtling
inexorably toward that final equation,
that final and bottom line.

Losing Battle

In a final desperate attempt
at survival, the sun sets
fire to the western sky.
Overblown, say my poet friends.
Cute, say my non-poet friends.
What does it mean? asks my neighbor.
How much will you get paid for it?
That's from my wife.

My father's an astronaut,
My son lies.

Regeneration

Don't wrestle elephants or apes.
Avoid undocumented gaps.
Don't Tarzan play on Mother's drapes.
Or battle cops with bottle caps.

Don't go looking for a fight
But don't go running from one.
Don't moon around all day and night.
Go find a special someone.

If hats are worn, they should be tipped
But not worn in the elevator.
Pants should normally be zipped
(exceptions will be noted later).

Mind these precepts, everyone—
Or at least as many as you can.
And when you are a man, my son,
Relay them to your son, my man.

Now I Lay Me Down to Sleep

When I feel the need to sleep
I lie down crumpled in a heap.

My body tired, worn and taxed.
It feels so good to be relaxed.

The arms of Morpheus have beckoned.
I'm fast asleep. FOR JUST A SECOND.

That's when I begin my twitching..
"Go to sleep, hon." (My wife, bitching.)

So I start my night-time movement.
Left side, right side. No improvement.

Face up, face down. Who's that joke? Me.
Again she wakes up, "Please don't poke me."

Can't lie still. My body's fluttering.
No need to tell you what she's muttering.

Legs all tangled. Arms akimbo.
While next to me my wife's in Limbo.

I count the sheep. They pass by singly.
And all this time my toes feel tingly.

Surely, think I, I will doze off.
Somewhere, some place, an alarm clock goes off.

Footsteps

When I was young (and now I'm old)
I was a rotten kid.
I never did what I was told
Or told them what I did.

But now I'm old and find this true—
My kids will very seldom
Tell me what they're going to do
Or do the things I tell them.

7

Very like a whale.

—Hamlet
Act III Scene 2

Bad Day at Black Rock

The cattle cackled.
The fowl mooed.

Rain Date

You saw the giraffes first.
Two heads. Heads held high.
High above the other animals.
What's up with that? she asked.
Great flood where they came from.
Where would that be? Curious. Not caring.
The Mideast. The Near East. Somewhere east.
Great, she said, but they better
not land here. They smell.
We watched them approach.
We need the rain, she said.
I need a raincoat, I said,
holding my nose.

Short Attention Span

The problem of being
        a 17-year
        locust
is trying to stay
        for 16 years
        focused.

An Epistle from Paul

This poem's for you, Babe.
The poem you always wanted.
A love poem.
Not light verse.
No silly rhymes.
Or sillier puns.
No hiding from true feelings
        behind a play on words.
No dactyls or anapests
        to throw you off stride.
Just a simple honest love poem
        to you, Babe.
To you, my dear.
My dear.
My ox.
My blue ox.

Bull!

It's Mindy the cow I am
And it's lust that I'm thinking of.
I didn't moo for you ma'am.
I, Mindy, mooed for love.

The Secret Life of Butterflies

The butterfly
will flutter by
and while fluttering
will be muttering
"I'd rather be Phyllis Diller
than a caterpillar."

Vegetarians

Mares eat oats
And does eat oats
And little lambs eat ivy.

And we eat them.

8

Doth it not show vilely in me to desire small beer?

—Henry IV Part 2
Act II Scene 2

Cravat Emptor

In the Nineties
I had nine ties
(of course).
But now it's a new millennium
And I don't have ennium
(remorse).

Benediction

I wanna be like Uncle Benny
He was one of those elegant gents
He never had a penny
He never had no sense.

Pillage, Rape, Plunder; Pillage, Rape, Plunder

There are no sloths
Among the Goths
And the Visigoths
Are busy Goths.

Excitement

Game seven.
Game's even!

Bend It Like Edmund

I'm pretty reliable
If you need someone pliable
Or would be if
I weren't so stiff.

Differential Calculus

It takes
two to
tango
but one
to tan.

Go figure.

Lost in Translation

Perdu

Id Est

(Ed ist?)

The id I'd like to be
Is (not very adventurously) me.

9

This is the news: he fishes, drinks and wastes.

—Antony and Cleopatra
Act I Scene 4

Live from the Sidewalk, It's Me!

I'm walking along the sidewalks where I live
in a hurry but too fast for my age
and weight and mission and I think
if I keep this up I'm going to drop dead
right here in River City but forget the
seventy-six trombones what I don't want
is fanfare.

                But what do I want I ask myself
besides not dropping dead. Well I want
to get where I'm going and don't ask where
that is because I forgot which is easy to do
at my age (and weight). Probably I want
to know the meaning of life although that
can wait until I get where I'm going which
may take a while because—as you may
have noticed—I'm slowing down a little
not to smell the roses mind you, it's just
that at my age and—well you know the rest.

Hey, here we are at the mailbox and damn!
there goes the mail truck.

A Lovely Day in the Neighborhood

I'm telling one of my neighbors about
my latest worry. That someday someone
will move next door to me and be one
of those guys who likes to overdecorate
their homes for Christmas. You know,
I tell him, with the plastic Santa Claus
and the Styrofoam snowmen—a whole
family of them—and reindeer, on the roof
probably, and lights, lots of lights,
green lights, blue lights, orange lights,
yellow lights, all flashing, and music,
loud music, piped from the house, day and
night, you know, all the favorites—
I saw Mama Kissing Santa Claus, the chipmunks,
Bing Crosby—and the sightseers in their
vans and pickups, gawking, stopping, blocking
my driveway, leaving garbage.

I stop to catch my breath and my neighbor
taps his specially blended tobacco from
his specially ordered meerschaum pipe,
puts his Mark Cross briefcase on the back
seat of his Jaguar and before he gets in
turns to me and says, listen, you want
something to worry about? The next time
I catch your goddam mutt taking a crap
in my wife's prize petunias, I'm going to
punch your fucking lights out.

Beaming

Miss Manners believes that an elegant
dinner party is not the venue to mention
your cancer, especially when Dr. Henry
Kissinger is the guest of honor. Miss
Manners is positive the other guests
are more interested in Mr. Kissinger's
views on the Mideast than your little
problem. Miss Manners must also
point out we are dealing with your
prostate, hardly a fit subject for
dinner conversation. She also wonders
if an account of your regimen
of daily radiation might dissuade
the good doctor from expounding
on his world views.

Miss Manners is reminded of the motto,
'For God, for Country and for
Yale' and wonders if you want to
be lumped with such anticlimactic
pronouncements. Miss Manners suggests
you beam quietly, listen avidly to our
esteemed guest, pass the rolls and,
in the spirit of the holidays, radiate joy.

Moonlighting

I'd like to be a walker-by.
I think I could do it.
It seems easy.
You just walk by in the background
of a TV show. For instance,
Jerry, George and Elaine are having lunch
at the restaurant and there's someone
standing at the cash register.
I could have done that. Stood there.
Or Scotty and Mr. Spock get in the elevator
of the Enterprise. And there is another
Vulcan already there. I could be that Vulcan.
Just don't make me try to speak Vulcan.
Walking by. Standing around. Blending
into the background. I could do it all.
After all.
I'm a poet.

A Musing

I finally get a hold of my Muse
and instead of inspiring me she
says give it up but I want a second
opinion and ask for Erato or
Calliope (I knew I didn't want
Euterpe and Terpsichore with
their same old song and dance)
but those 2 are busy giving poetry
readings at 2K a throw plus
expenses anyway Melpomene agrees
to see me next Tuesday although
it would have been fun to get
Clio then if I didn't get in-
spired I could say Clio
you're history but back to
the ranch house I have to
wait there all day Tuesday and
I have to take a vacation
day and finally at 4 o'clock
she shows up to tell me don't
quit your day job. What a
tragic muse.

Speaking for Ourselves, Ann

We're shy and standoffish
And sometimes outlandish.
As males, stylish
As Miles Standish.

Spring Song

I stopped to pee
against a tree
like a dogwood.

The Straight Skinny

To say that only I am fat,
To say that I am only fat,
To say only that I am fat,
To only say that I am fat,
Is not to say, however, that
They equally are definitive.

One statement says fat's mine alone.
One says no other trait I own,
One just has a plaintive tone,
And—overlooked and overblown—
One just splits the infinitive.

Tabled

It was an epiphany.
I know, I just can't say that.
I have to show it. Well,
look, listen. I'm sitting
in my cubicle when
I'm suddenly overwhelmed
by a sense of loss.

If I were an ancient Greek
I would have run naked
through the aisles shouting
Eureka! I have lost it. (Or
does it mean I have found it?)
But I'm not. Nor am I
an Ancient Mariner. No,
I'm an ancient programmer
staring at my computer
terminal reflecting
on this: I never
played enough
pingpong.

Shoot for the Moon

Did you know
that every time
you ejaculate
you release
enough sperm
to fertilize
every planet
in the universe?

All you have to do
Is raise your sights.

10

Exit, pursued by a bear.

—The Winter's Tale
Act III Scene 3

On Becoming a Famous Poet

From a little no-name
To a little-known name.

Shadows, 9–10–200

In the morning the shadows reach across
the Hudson, side by side. At 10, they pause
for coffee, then glide up the river. They
will arrive soon at the George Washington Bridge
and cross back to Manhattan. They will go
their separate ways for lunch in Central Park and join
up at the East River. A lazy afternoon
In Queens and Brooklyn. And as the sun
is captured by New Jersey they stretch out
over Long Island and blend into the darkness.

They are with us still.

The War of the Roses Comes to an Exciting Anti-Climax

Wear red
You're dead.
Wear white
You're dead.

Time and Tide

Many a castaway
Has passed away
Writing "Help" in the sand
And "Help" and "Help" and

An Island Entire of Myself

I said, There is no God.
He said, That's fine with me.
And I? Another clod
Washed away by the sea.

Spoiler

Here's the story.
Memento mori.

The Party's Over

Galaxyz

11

Make no noise. Make no noise. Draw the curtains—

—King Lear
Act II Scene 6

About the Author

Edmund Conti has been writing poetry (OK, verse) for over 70 years which is a long time for a young man. He got off on the wrong foot (an iamb, maybe) by trying to rhyme ignite and lignite. He didn't realize this for another 20 years so he just kept on writing. So what hath Ed wrought? Well, when he was counting there were at least 500 published poems. There seemed to be fewer poems when he stopped counting. (Moral: never stop counting.) He has poems published in *Light, Lighten-up Online, Abbey, Bogg, The Lyric, Sow's Ear, Asses of Parnassus,* and others modesty prevents him from mentioning. (Oh, all right, *Slapdash Hackery Factory, Folly, Rotary Dial, Cat's Eye, Z Miscellaneous, Hobo Stew Review* (There, are you satisfied?))

Conti is also the author of *Just So You Know* from Kelsay Books. Among his other chapbooks—*Quiblets, The Ed C. Scrolls, Eddies, Hic Haiku Hoc, Greatest Hits, O Fractal Day, Words and Music by Edmund Conti, Wax and Wayne* (with Wayne Hogan), *Eb and Flo* (with Wayne Hogan). Don't worry, none are available except for *Just So You Know.* Just so you know.

Conti was once a featured poet for *Light Magazine.* He won the first Willard Espy Foundation Prize for Light Verse in 2001. He read at the Waterloo Poetry Festival in New Jersey, mostly because he lived in the area. Location pays.

www.ingramcontent.com/pod-product-compliance
Lightning Source LLC
Chambersburg PA
CBHW070500090426
42735CB00012B/2626